ROOTS UNCOVERED

Uncovering the Root Causes of Unhealthy Hair

QUANISHA WHITFIELD

Roots uncovered

Uncovering the Root Causes of Unhealthy Hair

Copyright © 2021 Quanisha Whitfield

All rights reserved. Printed in the United States of America. No part of this book may be used or reproduced in any manner whatsoever without written permission except in the case of brief quotations in critical articles or reviews.

Cover Design, Typesetting, Book Layout by
Enger Lanier Taylor for In Due Season Publishing

Published By: In Due Season Publishing
Huntsville, Alabama
indueseasonpublishing@gmail.com
www.indueseasonpublishing.com

ISBN-13: 978-1-970057-11-9
ISBN-10: 1-970057-11-4

Website: hannorahaircare.com
Facebook: Hannora Hair Care
Instagram: Hannora Hair Care

DISCLAIMER:

This book is not intended as a substitute for the medical advice of physicians. The reader should consult a physician in matters relating to his/her health and particularly with respect to any symptoms that may require diagnosis or medical attention regarding your hair and/or hair loss. The author and publisher do not assume and hereby disclaim any liability to any party for any loss, damage, or side effects of any kind related to the following information in this book. It is strictly for informational purposes only.

- This regimen requires your participation.

- The information presented does not seek to discredit any medical practices, church, psychological or religious doctrine.

- This strategy does not replace the need to seek a professional diagnosis or treatment by a Dermatologist or Trichologist.

- This strategy does not replace the need for you to regularly see a professional Barber or Cosmetologist.

- All hair loss is not the same. Therefore treatment and regimens will vary.

- None of these strategies work alone. It is recommended that you combine them for the best results.

- This information is for your general knowledge, to give insight into hair issues and possible solutions.

- We are not responsible for a person's issue, symptoms, diagnosis, or their healing.

- There are no guarantees that any person's issues will be resolved or prevented.

- The results will vary based on application, consistency, determination, faith, and belief system.

- The author reserves the right to revise this information as the depth of understanding increases.

CONTENTS

Introduction

Busting Myths 112

Maintaining Your Roots 201

Fitness & Nutritional Roots 29

Spiritual Roots 32

Healthy Roots 41

Hair Declarations/Women 43

Hair Declarations/Men 47

Hair Declarations/Children 51

Prayer 53

Definitions 60

Food Guide 65

Oil Guide 68

Author Bio 70

References

INTRODUCTION

Hello Friend!

I hope you and your hair are prospering. If not, I hope that your hair and everything concerning you begins to prosper and be in good health after reading this book.

I know! You have heard it all before. You have tried tons of products and remedies, receiving little to no results or maybe even terrible results. But wait, this is different! Throughout my years of being a Cosmetologist, I have discovered something I believe is profound. Many clients have been trying to treat their hair issues topically only when the problem is deeper than the scalp. So, I came up with a strategy to pair with a topical regimen that can help produce positive results in little time.

This book will help you uncover the root causes of unhealthy hair and discover the possible solution to the problem. This information partnered with your participation, determination, discipline, consistency, and faith will be a significant factor in the results you receive.

1

BUSTING MYTHS

I have chosen 10 of many myths to debunk. These myths are in no particular order.

1. Never get a relaxer!

The truth is, getting relaxers are not necessarily harmful. Hair fibers are made of elements such as carbon, oxygen, nitrogen, hydrogen, and sulfur. These elements create side bonds. There are three types of side bonds, but I will focus on two, which are Hydrogen bonds and Disulfide bonds. Hydrogen bonds can easily be broken by water and heat, causing what should be temporary changes to the hair strand's shape. A few examples of the ways that hydrogen bonds can be broken include a simple shampoo, humidity, flat iron, or roller set. Each of these cause the hair to temporarily change from its natural state yet causing no damage to the hair.

However, you must be careful with flat ironing or blowing out the hair. Too much heat or constant heat application can lead to permanent damage to the curl pattern causing the hair to not revert back to its original state.

Now, disulfide bonds are the protein structures of the hair. It is the strongest bond and cannot be broken by water or heat. Chemical processes such as relaxers, perms, and color break these bonds. This causes a permanent change to the hair strand.

While permanent changes occur due to relaxers, it does not mean the hair is unhealthy. Many people have had bad experiences with relaxers and have encouraged others not to get them. Someone's bad experience does not mean that will happen for someone else and vice versa. I believe the best way to go is "chemical-free," but I am not totally against chemicals, especially if they are being done by a trustworthy, reputable professional. Here are a few tips on getting relaxers:

- Find a reputable cosmetologist to perform the process for you.
- Make sure your edges and scalp are based on some type of scalp protector.

- Do not allow the relaxer to stay on the hair until it is "bone straight." It can result in brittle hair, dry hair, breakage, or baldness.
- The hair should have some type of wave left to it when wet.
- If you are getting a relaxer retouch, ONLY relax the new growth. DO NOT relax hair that has already been processed because it could lead to over processing and hair damage.
- Deep condition with a protein conditioner to help restore some of the protein that was broken down by the chemical.
- Try to use a mild relaxer. Most people do not need super.
- Try to go at least 12 weeks between relaxers.
- People with high porosity hair should refrain from getting relaxers.

2. **You should not use oil or grease in or on your hair.**

The truth is, you need to add oil and/or grease to your hair, even if it is only twice a month, depending on the hairstyle and porosity. Our hair is made up of some oils, and our scalp produces oil, but it is not always enough to protect or penetrate the hair the way it needs to. Water is our friend but has the potential of becoming an enemy if overused on the hair. Too much water can lead to hygral fatigue. This causes cuticle lifting, brittleness, tangling, and ultimately breakage. There has to be balance.

Some Causes of Hygral Fatigue:

- The hair constantly going from wet to dry
- Daily washes without adding a penetrating and protective oil or grease
- Overnight deep conditioning too often
- Deep conditioning longer than the recommended time
- Using products that lack proteins

You may be experiencing Hygral Fatigue if the hair:

- Feels really rough and dry once it dries
- Is really soft or gummy feeling when wet
- Limp
- Frizzy
- Tangling
- Does not hold a curl well
- The hair stretches then breaks

Solution:

- Try avoiding water for a while and adding oil with protein such as coconut oil and hemp seed oil.
- Add protein in moderation because, unfortunately, too much protein can be harmful to the hair as well.

- If you do not see positive changes, you may have to cut off the damaged hair.

Prevent Hygral Fatigue:

- Pretreat hair with a protective, protein-filled oil that will coat the hair
- Pre-poo with oil two days before shampoo day
- Do not constantly wet the hair

3. **You do not need to go to a cosmetologist.**

The truth is, you might. YouTube is a great resource and has helped many of us, myself included. However, sometimes no matter how hard I try to do what they do, I fail because some areas they teach on are simply not my expertise. When you start becoming concerned about your hair, I suggest going to a cosmetologist to see if the problem has a simple fix.

Why go to a reputable Licensed Cosmetologist:

- To be sure, you are not treating your hair wrong.
- So that you do not add to the problem instead of eliminating it
- To eliminate spending or wasting lots of money in trial and error
- To get on a healthy hair regimen
- To get a referral to a dermatologist or trichologist if the cosmetologist believes medical attention is necessary for the issue

ROOTS UNCOVERED

4. You do not need to seek a dermatologist or trichologist.

The truth is, you might. Some scalp issues are beyond home remedies and even weekly hair appointments. If these issues are diagnosed early, and treatment begins early enough, it could end the problem. We often allow problems to linger, causing prolonged suffering or even permanent damage.

Signs you may need to seek a dermatologist or trichologist:

- Extremely dry scalp
- Large flakes on the scalp
- Bleeding scalp
- Pus filled bumps on the scalp
- Red or white scaly bumps on the scalp
- Extreme hair loss for no apparent reason
- Thinning or hair loss by the entire strand, not just breakage
- Pain, severe itching, or extreme tenderness to the scalp
- Possible allergic reaction to hair products

5. If you cannot pronounce it, you should not use it.

The truth is, this is false.

Say this with me, Melaleuca Alternifolia. Melaaaluu... Ok, I can't say it either. However, I love to use it. It's organic, an essential oil, and very beneficial to the hair and scalp. It is tea tree oil. There you have it; just research it if you cannot pronounce it. Do not miss out on something that could benefit you all because it doesn't look familiar. Whew! That will preach!

6. Alcohol in hair products are bad for the hair.

The truth is, this is true to an extent. There are two types of alcohols, drying alcohols and fatty alcohols. We want to try to stay away from drying alcohols. However, if you cannot, do not panic. Most times, the alcohol used in the product is very low to help preserve the product. The amount is so little it will be diluted by the other contents in the product and most likely cause no harm to the hair unless it is used regularly or excessively.

Now let's get to the fatty alcohols. These alcohols are very healthy for the hair. They are great for smoothing and moisturizing the hair.

7. Trimming ends is cutting the length off of your hair.

The truth is, NOT cutting your ends results in having to cut off the length of your hair because it will be damaged. You MUST have your ends trimmed regularly, at least once every six weeks.

Trim ends regularly to avoid:
- Breakage
- Fly-aways

ROOTS UNCOVERED

- Tangling
- Dryness
- Having to get a hair cut instead of a trim

8. Dirty hair makes your hair grow.

The truth is, this is false. Dirty hair does not make your hair grow, but low manipulation causes you to retain length. Your natural sebum has time to produce and travel down the hair shaft, which conditions and protects the hair strands.

9. You have to wash your hair weekly.

The truth is, this is false. You do not have to wash your hair weekly or biweekly. If you can go for eight weeks without a shampoo, go for it! The hair is best when it is left alone! If you experience product build-up, dandruff build-up, or smelly hair, please shampoo your hair when you need to. However, it is not a requirement to wash your hair every week.

10. Braids, twists, crochets, and other protective styles are bad for your hair.

The truth is, this is false. These protective styles are not bad for your hair. They are actually great for retaining the length of the hair. However, depending on the hair's condition, it may not be a wise decision to get a protective style that is heavy or requires a lot of tension. No matter how healthy your hair is, do not get these

QUANISHA WHITFIELD

styles too tight. They can be done neatly without pulling and breaking the hair.

2

MAINTAINING YOUR ROOTS

There is much more to maintaining your hair than just shampooing, conditioning, and styling. The ingredients in the products, personal hygiene, and consistency all play a part in the hair maintenance journey. Here, I will talk about the basics needs of maintaining healthy hair.

1. Learn your hair.

Your hair speaks daily. You must listen to it. It is important to pay attention to how your hair responds to certain environments, weather, products, regimens, styles, and even hairstylists. What works for others may not work for you, and that is ok. The hair's response is contingent upon many things, especially your hair's porosity, texture, and density. Everyone's hair is different.

Your hair will let you know what product and regimen makes it happy. A reputable Licensed Cosmetologist can assist in this process.

Happy Responses:

Moist
Bouncy
Shiny
Smooth

Sad Responses:

Dry
Brittle
Tangling
Gummy Feeling
Limp

2. Retain the length of your hair.

There are three phases of hair growth; anagen, catagen, and telogen. The science behind retaining length is the ability to prolong the anagen stage. Many people believe their hair cannot grow past a certain length because their hair has stopped at the same place for years. When the hair is healthy with no thinning, hormonal changes, or medical issues, the issue is not a lack of growth. It's the lack of length retention.

Here are some ways to retain length:

- Break the bad habit of twirling and playing in your hair. Keep your hands out of your hair.
- If your hair and scalp permit, wear protective styles for weeks at a time. The less manipulation, the better chance at retaining length.
- Apply condition or oil when taking down protective styles
- Gently take down protective styles
- Do not yank or comb through the small knots at the end of your hair. Cut them to prevent splitting the hair up the shaft.
- Do not excessively blow dry and flat iron your hair
- When flat ironing, do not use high heat, use heat protectant, and try not to run the flat iron over each subsection of hair more than two times to protect the hair from losing its original elasticity or breaking due to heat damage.
- Chase a heat resistant comb with the flatiron directly behind it to eliminate having to constantly flat iron the hair to straighten the hair.

- Wear a silk bonnet as often as you can, especially in the house and vehicle. Wearing a bonnet helps prevent friction against the ends of your hair. When your hair is out or down, it is constantly rubbing against your clothes or even the seat of your vehicle. Keep your hair covered as much as possible.
- Keep ends trimmed by a reputable Cosmetologist. The type of shears used to perform a trim matters. It is important to go to a professional stylist who uses professional shears and not the shears from the hair supply store or regular scissors. Furthermore, the ends of the hair are the oldest parts of the hair strand and can be very fragile. Therefore, they cannot be avoided, but they can be maintained well. When trimmed frequently, they are trimmed at minimal length, usually less than an inch. This prevents breakage and allows you to see length retention.
- Use DHT blocking ingredients: DHT (derived from testosterone) is a vital sex steroid and hormone in the body that can cause damage to hair health and growth if there is an excess amount. Excess DHT is one of the leading causes of hair loss in men but can also affect women. Fortunately, there are ways to slow the hair loss process and possibly

stop it. Here are some topical, natural DHT blocking ingredients to look for in products:

- Saw Palmetto Oil
- Pumpkin Seed Oil
- Stinging Nettle Oil
- Tea Tree Oil
- Soy Bean Oil
- Lavender Oil

3. Properly Moisturize Your Hair

Properly moisturizing the hair can be a challenging task for some. Many have tried different avenues to keep hair moisturized and have failed at it over and over again. There is more to moisturizing than putting in a leave-in conditioner or oiling the scalp. There is a method to this. I learned this method from Chemist Tonya Lane, also known as Curly Chemistry, on YouTube. Listen! Please subscribe to her channel! You will be so glad you did! Plus, she explains this method better than I will ever be able to.

P.M.P. Method
This stands for penetrate, moisture, protect.

- You need a penetrating oil that will go inside of the hair strand while blocking excessive water entry.
- Then you'll need a moisturizing agent that will actually moisturize the hair.
- Then you'll need a protectant oil that will seal the cuticle, lock in moisture, and protect the inside of the strand.
- Types of Penetrating Oils: Coconut Oil and Babassu Oil
- Types of Moisturizing Agents: Leave-In Conditioners or liquid type moisturizers with glycerin or aloe in it.
- Types of Protecting Oils: Avocado Oil and Castor Oil
- Again, follow *Curly Chemistry* on YouTube to learn more.

4. Seek Professional Care for Your Scalp and Hair

Professional Hair Care is important no matter how much you think you know about your hair. There are many professional, reputable cosmetologists and hairstylists worldwide who would love to service you. Take the time and research to find a stylist to go to at least four times a year to ensure that your hair stays in good health. It is worth the investment.

When looking for a hairstylist, remember your goal. Is your goal to obtain and maintain healthy hair? Is your goal to have someone install a flawless sew-in? Is your goal to have the straightest blow out ever? Is your goal to get some bomb feed in braids? This is important to note because the stylist who specifies in helping you obtain and maintain healthy hair may not believe in giving you feed in braids because of the possibility of breaking and pulling of the hair and edges. The stylist who does the flawless sew-in may not consider the natural hair's health and the possible harm that too much tension could cause. This does not mean the stylist does not care for your hair. Their specialty is in a different area, and they choose to stay in their lane. However, some stylists can do all of these things well. So, be sure to do your research.

Furthermore, do not be ashamed to seek medical advice. Dermatologists and trichologists have much more insight into more advanced issues of the hair and scalp. They have access to provide medicated treatments that could stop, heal, or reverse an issue.

Most importantly, honesty is imperative! Be honest with yourself about the condition of your hair and scalp. Be honest with your stylist about what you are putting in your hair and your hair maintenance routine. Finally, be honest with your dermatologist and trichologist about your hair care routine, hair genealogy, and all other questions they may ask.

3

FITNESS & NUTRITIONAL ROOTS

Healthy living is necessary for healthy hair. It is imperative that you begin to beautify what is within just as you desire to beautify your outer appearance.

1. Exercising helps promote hair growth.

One essential part of the hair growth process is the blood flow in the scalp. Exercising gets the heart pumping and causes the blood to flow and circulate vastly. Also, your scalp produces sweat when you exercise. Sweat helps unclog hair follicles and opens up pores in the scalp, releasing build-up and allowing new hair to come through.

Recommended Exercises to serve this purpose:

- Walking
- Running
- Dancing
- Hold head down while massaging the scalp

2. Hair grows from the inside of our bodies.

Being that hair grows from the inside of the body, what you put in your body matters. The food you eat matters more than you may know. Eating healthy food assists in healthy hair growth. It also aids in a healthy body and prolonged life. Detoxing and fasting can also be beneficial if your body and lifestyle permits.

Indulge in foods that are rich in:

- Protein
- Iron
- Zinc
- Calcium
- Biotin
- Lycopene
- Drink PLENTY of water

Stay away from:

- Complex Carbs (Starches and Sugars)
- Refined Carbs

3. Medications can affect your hair.

Many medications affect the condition of the hair, but one prevalent one is blood pressure medication. These meds often cause thinning or balding in the very top of the head. Eating healthy and exercising consistently could lead to lower doses of the medication or coming off of the medications altogether. *However, please do not stop taking your prescribed medications. Consult with your doctor to establish a health and wellness regimen, set a goal, and execute it well.*

4

SPIRITUAL ROOTS

I am sure you have seen or heard several commercials advertising solutions to hair loss. There have been ads for different oils, laser hair combs, Minoxidil, Finasteride, and many other treatments. These are all great topical solutions, but they are not always effective. I have discovered a treatment for a rarely discussed cause of hair damage and hair loss. This chapter will uncover what I believe is one of the most overlooked causes of hair loss: an unhealthy soul.

Some of the hair issues people experience are not because of a lack of maintenance, bad hygiene, unhealthy diet, or sedentary lifestyle. It is the outward manifestation of a soul issue. Now whether you are a

ROOTS UNCOVERED

reader of the Bible, a believer of it, or a Christian at all, I would encourage you to not skip over this part as it may be what you have needed all along in your hair recovery journey. So let's dig into the scriptures.

Disclaimer: Although these scriptures have a biblical interpretation, I believe there is a further revelation in each of them.

Psalm 139:13-16

¹³ You made all the delicate, inner parts of my body and knit me together in my mother's womb. ¹⁴ Thank you for making me so wonderfully complex! Your workmanship is marvelous—how well I know it. ¹⁵ You watched me as I was being formed in utter seclusion, as I was woven together in the dark of the womb. ¹⁶ You saw me before I was born. Every day of my life was recorded in your book. Every moment was laid out before a single day had passed.

I opened with this scripture to affirm you and let you know that you are not an experiment. In fact, you were made and crafted intentionally, on purpose, and for a purpose. God loves every part of you and thinks the most precious thoughts about you. Your skin color, complexion, eyes, nose, every dimple, and blemish is just the way He intended for it to be. Even the color and texture of your hair was intentional. Now that you understand just how unique and wonderful you are, let's dig a little deeper.

Luke 12:7

And the very hairs on your head are all numbered. So don't be afraid; you are more valuable to God than a whole flock of sparrows.

God was so meticulous in creating you that he even knows the numbers of hairs upon your head. The fact that He says the "very" hairs on your head are "all" numbered makes me believe there should be an abundance of hair upon the head. He follows by saying, "Don't be afraid." This lets me know that there are things that will try to come to discourage you and make you afraid. After giving the instruction, He follows with this affirmation, "You are more valuable to God than a whole flock of sparrows."

I'm led to believe people or things will come to make you feel rejected or less than, ultimately leading to fear of ridicule or not fitting in. If you have experienced ridicule of any sort, you may feel like a failure at some point in your life, began to hate yourself, and have become afraid of trying again or trying something new. However, God wants you to not fear because you are too valuable for Him to allow anything or circumstance to overtake you.

Luke 21:16-18

Even those closest to you-your parents, brothers, relatives, and friends- will betray you. They will even kill some of you. And everyone will hate you because you are my followers. But not a hair on your head will perish!

According to this scripture, I believe there is a possibility of being hurt, hated, betrayed, or persecuted by those close to you. Even though this may happen, He tells you that not a hair on your head will perish. So I ask, why is it that the hairs on many of our heads are perishing? I believe the pain caused by family and friends may have led to anger, rage, unforgiveness, stress, and lack of trust in God. Everyone has been hurt, sometimes repeatedly. However, not all of us have forgiven and healed. You may even believe you are healed but have actually just buried the pain. I will add this as well, anytime you have gone through a healing process without the inclusion of God, Jesus, and Holy Spirit, I can guarantee you, you are not completely healed. Choosing to hold on to hurt, pain, and disappointments can result in hair loss issues, scalp diseases, and many other ailments. Be reminded that no matter what has ever happened, if you are alive and reading this today, you have already witnessed God as your protector, healer, and comforter. As long as you trust Him FULLY, and not a hair on your head shall perish, again.

Exodus 20:5-6

You must not bow down to them or worship them, for I, the Lord your God, am a jealous God who will not tolerate your affection for any other gods. I lay the sin of the parents upon their children; the entire family is affected- even children in the third and fourth generations of those who reject me. But I lavish unfailing love for a thousand generations on those who love me and obey me.

Generational curses enter in by someone willingly sinning against God without true repentance. There are different types of generational curses, such as sinful patterns, destructive behaviors, faulty mindsets, and physical ailments. When we have sinful ways or strongholds, we pass this to our family members and down to the generations after us if we do not decide to break them! This is why we see different issues being passed to children, grandchildren, great-grandchildren, and so on. Some patterns that may occur in your family line may be linked to a generational curse.

Some examples are:

- Alcoholism
- Divorce
- Children out of wedlock
- Poverty
- Anxiety
- Miscarriages
- Heart Disease
- Cancer
- Alopecia

This is important to address because I believe many things we have accepted as hereditary diseases or ailments are actually generational curses. Many people have been diagnosed with androgenetic alopecia. According to MedlinePlus, it is estimated that 80 million people in the United States alone suffer from androgenetic alopecia and starts as early as one's teenage years. Other hair and scalp diseases may have been passed down throughout generations or maybe even started with you. While treatments may help with this issue, I believe the cycle of hair loss and all the other problems can end permanently. If you think you or someone you know deals with any of these issues, take the time to check your family history, read your Bible, pray, get deliverance, and make the decision to set your whole bloodline free! Your children and grandchildren will not have to suffer because you decided to break the curse! Oh Yes!

Here are a few other characteristics to check for in your family line:

- Anger
- Rage
- Unforgiveness (Holding Grudges)
- Stress
- Self Hatred
- Self Rejection
- Depression
- Isolation

ROOTS UNCOVERED

The things listed could be the reason behind the sins that are prominent in your family. For example, depression may be the reason behind alcoholism. Self-hatred may be the reason behind fornication. Fear and unforgiveness may be manifesting as androgenetic alopecia. So, go deep to try to get to the root of the issue.

3 John 1:2

Beloved, I wish <u>above all things</u> that you may prosper and be in health, even as your soul prospers.

God is concerned about your entire being. He says above all things He desires that you prosper and be in good health just as your soul prospers. Just as much as He desires for your soul to be whole, so does He desire for your body and everything else concerning you to be whole. That includes your hair. After all, your hair is a part of you. He cares so much about every aspect of you, inside and out! Make it a goal to take pride in caring for yourself inwardly just as much as you do outwardly so that you may prosper and be in good health, even as your soul prospers.

I pray you take heed to this chapter. I believe that every part of you is of great value. I genuinely care about every aspect of you, and so does God. I challenge you to do the work. Do not be afraid if you do not understand. A lack of understanding is sometimes an invitation to grab a shovel and dig deeper until you understand. We are spirit beings who have a soul that occupies a body. That means at the core of who we are lies a spirit and soul that must be adequately nourished, or we will pay for it in another part of our bodies and lives.

5

HEALTHY ROOTS

Now that you have the information you need to obtain and maintain healthy roots start applying what you have discovered. Using these strategies can be challenging to start, but you can do this if you are truly ready to see a change in your hair and your entire life.

Keys To Having Healthy Roots:
- Read the material thoroughly
- Accept that changes may need to be made in your life rather naturally or spiritually
- Do Not Resist Change
- Resist Fear
- Decide to Improve

- Set SMART goals (specific, measurable, attainable, relevant, timely)
- Gradually make the necessary changes to see positive results
- Journal your progress
- Stay Positive
- Find Joy in the process
- Remain Focused
- Remain Determined
- Be Consistent
- Pray
- Believe
- Follow Through

6

HAIR DECLARATIONS
FOR WOMEN

I expect to see positive results.

I love myself.

I love my hair.

I come out of agreement with every lie that I have believed about myself.

I do not hate my hair.

I am grateful for my hair.

I am not what others say about me.

I am beautiful.

QUANISHA WHITFIELD

My hair is beautiful.

I am beautiful inside and out.

I am valuable.

My hair is healthy.

I am healthy.

I am important.

My hair is important.

I do not worship my hair, but I do maintain it well because God cares about the health and prosperity of everything concerning me.

I am stress-free.

I let go of anything that would cause me to lose my character, peace, mind, money, or hair.

My environment is stress-free.

My home is peaceful.

I find peace within myself.

I am worthy of happiness, peace, love, and joy.

I am whole physically, emotionally, financially, mentally,

ROOTS UNCOVERED

socially, spiritually.

I am confident.

I am uniquely and wonderfully made.

I am special and extraordinary.

I have a sound mind filled with positive thoughts.

I am decided, determined, and dedicated.

I choose to forgive all those who hurt me intentionally and unintentionally.

I choose to let go of rage, anger, bitterness, and unforgiveness.

I choose to heal and be made whole.

I am a generational curse breaker.

I can do this.

I will do this.

I have faith in myself.

I have faith in my hair.

Most of all, I have faith in God.

My hair will grow at an accelerated rate.

QUANISHA WHITFIELD

My scalp is healed.

My mind is healed.

My heart is healed.

My soul is healed.

I will make the necessary changes in my diet, hygiene, and lifestyle to achieve my hair goals.

My hair, My crown, and glory will be revived, restored, and refined.

May my hair prosper, even as my soul prospers!

7

HAIR DECLARATIONS
For Men

I am a king.

I am a man of honor.

I was created on purpose.

I am full of purpose.

I am a man of vision who is focused.

I come out of agreement with every lie I have believed about myself.

I am not what others say about me.

I am valued.

QUANISHA WHITFIELD

I am responsible, dedicated, and determined.

I am healthy.

I will make the necessary changes to achieve the results I want to see physically, financially, emotionally, socially, mentally, and spiritually.

I am stress-free.

I let go of anything that would cause me to lose my character, peace, mind, money, or hair.

My environment is stress-free.

My home is peaceful.

I find peace within myself.

I am forgiving and understanding.

I choose to forgive those who hurt me intentionally and unintentionally.

I choose to let go of rage, anger, bitterness, and unforgiveness.

I choose to heal and be made whole.

I am a generational curse breaker.

ROOTS UNCOVERED

I can do this.

I will do this.

I have faith in myself.

I have faith in my hair and beard.

Most of all, I have faith in God.

My hair and beard will grow long and full at an accelerated rate.

I maintain my hair and beard well.

I maintain myself well.

I maintain my finances and relationships well.

I look good, smell good, and feel good.

I am humble.

I do not worship my hair, beard, looks, or finances, but I do maintain them well because God cares about the health and prosperity of everything concerning me.

My intentions and motives are pure.

QUANISHA WHITFIELD

My scalp is healed.

My mind is healed.

My heart is healed.

My soul is healed.

I am becoming a new man, inside and out.

May my hair prosper, even as my soul prospers!

8

HAIR DECLARATIONS
FOR CHILDREN

I am amazing.

My hair looks amazing.

I am unique.

My differences are a gift to the world.

My hair is different.

I love and embrace my hair.

My hair is healthy.

My hair will grow long, thick, and strong.

My mom and dad love my hair.

My mom and dad love me.

QUANISHA WHITFIELD

I love me.

I love everything about me.

Most importantly, God loves me.

I am valued.

I am happy.

I am full of joy.

I am fearfully and wonderfully made.

May my hair prosper, even as my soul prospers!

9

PRAYERS

I feel as if I would be doing you a disservice if I gave you these tools without introducing you to the one who ultimately gave them to me. His name is Jesus. I invite you to pray this prayer aloud from your heart if you desire to give your life to Christ. I believe in faith that God will meet you right where you are right now.

Salvation Prayer

Dear Lord Jesus, Son of God, I know that I am a sinner, and I ask for your forgiveness. I believe you died on the cross for my sins, rose from the dead, and are coming back for me. I invite you to come into my heart and my life. I submit my life to you this day. I want to trust and follow you. I want to get to know you and your ways. I accept you, Jesus, as my Savior and Lord of my life. I confess with my mouth and believe in my heart; I am saved. I am a child of God. I am a citizen of the Kingdom of Heaven. In Jesus Name. Amen.

Healing Prayer

Our Father, who art in Heaven; You are the God of the Bible. You are God Almighty. You are the only true and living God. You are my creator, deliverer, healer, miracle worker, and Great Physician. May your Kingdom come, and your will be done on earth as it is in Heaven!

Father, I ask that you forgive me for my sins. Forgive me for all sins known and unknown that I have committed. Forgive me for dishonoring, grieving, and doing things that I know were unpleasing to you. Forgive me, Lord, for not loving myself and not embracing the things you took your precious time to create. Forgive me for not appreciating my eyes, nose, hair, lips, and everything else about me that you fearfully and wonderfully made. Forgive me for comparing myself to others. Forgive me for not walking in confidence and not wearing my hair in confidence because of fear of what others would say. Forgive me for believing the lies that others said about me instead of standing on and believing your word that is forever true. Forgive me for all the times that I spoke

ROOTS UNCOVERED

against or talked about your beautiful sons and daughters. Forgive me for any time I ridiculed another human being about anything, even when I was a young child or teenager. Forgive me for the times I gossiped or laughed at someone who was experiencing hair loss, skin disease, scalp disease, stunted hair growth, or other issues. Forgive me for laughing or gossiping about someone because of their hair texture, density, or hair color. Forgive me for ever cursing another human being. Forgive me for cursing any hairstylist, cosmetologist, dermatologist, trichologist who failed to meet my expectations. Forgive me for not forgiving those who left, hurt, backstabbed, betrayed, ridiculed, failed, or violated me. Forgive me, God, for not forgiving myself for things I've done in my past. Forgive me for mistreating my body, my temple. Forgive me for not eating well and maintaining my body well. Forgive me, Lord, for the wrong things I have done that I cannot even think of. Cleanse me from all unrighteousness, all ungodliness, and give me strength, wisdom, and boldness to never return to these ways.

Now, God, I thank you for a clean slate, a new day, and new mercies. I thank you for my life, for my family, friends, and loved ones. I thank you for what you have done in my life thus far and the marvelous things you continue to do. I am grateful for the hair I have, the body I possess, and the tools to maintain it well. Thank you, Lord, for the resources, courage, strength, consistency, grace, and wisdom you are giving me to steward all things well. Thank you, Father, for your redemptive love, deliverance power, and healing power. Thank you for loving me so much that, above all things, you desire for me to prosper and be in good health even as my soul prospers.

Therefore, I declare and decree that everything about me and around me shall prosper even as my soul prospers. God, it is your desire that my money, business, home, environment, family, bloodline, health, and even my hair prosper. I declare and decree by the power of the Holy Ghost that I am stress-free, drug-free, alcohol-free, obesity free, addiction-free, affliction free, pain-free, disease-free, poverty-free, free from hair loss, free from hate, and free from unforgiveness.

I am free from all things that do not align with your nature and your will for my life. I declare and decree that sickness, disease, and disorders are far from me. I am free from alopecia, androgenetic alopecia, psoriasis, rosacea, vitiligo, eczema, hives, and inflammation! I am free from ringworms, fungus, bacteria, parasites, and

ROOTS UNCOVERED

lice. I command all flakiness, dryness, tenderness, sores, rashes, blisters, and scabs to be healed now in Jesus' name! Father reverse, all hair loss and hair thinning now! I am loosed from every dermal, epidermal, and sebaceous gland disorder.

I command hair follicles to open up. I command blood to circulate properly. I command the hair to go through the Anagen Stage, Catagen stage, and telogen stage properly. I command the anagen stage to be maximized, extended, and prolonged. I command baldness to go! I command hair to grow in the frontal region, mid-scalp region, vertex transition point, crown, and nape. I have no hair missing in Jesus' name! Grow Hair Grow! May the healing power of your blood work in the areas where treatment was ineffective. Perform a miracle where I once thought or believed there was no treatment. For you can do what no medication, doctor, or hair regimen can do.

I break off the spirit of lack, laziness, stagnation, and procrastination off of my life! I declare and decree that I will make the necessary changes for my health to thrive, my hair to thrive, my finances to thrive, and my family to thrive. Everything must thrive! God, I need discipline; help me to be disciplined and consistent in Jesus' name.

QUANISHA WHITFIELD

I break every death sentence against my life. I command all death to dreams, hope, joy, healthy relationships, healthy living, red blood cells, white blood cells, and hair follicles to be reversed! You shall come alive! You shall live again! I command you to wake up! Open up! Dead things come alive, be healed, be restored, and made new!

I break the bondage of witchcraft, word curses, and generational curses off of my family and off of my bloodline. I overthrow every vex and hex that could affect the condition of my health and my hair. I break off everything that is hindering my hair from prospering and my soul from prospering.

I declare and decree that every demonic altar, generational curse, and form of bondage that has been shattered, broken, eradicated, dismantled, emptied out, uprooted, torn down, and erased is replaced with your unconditional love. May your love fill every void and empty place within my heart and my soul. May your peace and wisdom fill my mind! Holy Spirit endow me, overtake me, and make me brand new.

Now, God, I declare and decree that I am blessed. My house is blessed. My finances are blessed. My mind, body, and soul are blessed. My loved ones are blessed.

ROOTS UNCOVERED

My enemies are blessed. Everything I touch from this day forth is blessed, including my hair. Everything in me and around me is prospering and in good health, even as my soul prospers. In Jesus Name. Amen.

DEFINITIONS

Anagen Phase- The growing phase of the hair growth cycle. Hair can stay in this active phase of growth from anywhere between two and six years.

Androgenetic Alopecia- Hereditary Hair loss

Biotin- A B vitamin that helps maintain hair, nails, and skin

Catagen Phase- The transitional part of the cycle and lasts for around two to three weeks. In this stage, hair growth stops and is no longer active or able to grow.

Cosmetologist- A person who is licensed to perform non-medical cosmetic and beauty treatments

Dandruff - The dead skin on a person's scalp or in the hair. The accumulation of dandruff on the scalp is known as "dandruff build up."

Density- The number of hairs on a person's head per square inch. This is how thickness or thinness is determined.

Dermatologist- A medical doctor qualified to diagnose and treat all skin issues, including the scalp

ROOTS UNCOVERED

DHT- Dihydrotestosterone. A sex steroid is derived from testosterone responsible for the development of male primary sex characters but is also found in women.

Disulfide Bonds- Tertiary structure of the protein in the hair that can be broken by chemical processes. This is a permanent change to the hair.

Drying Alcohols- Alcohols found in products that help the hair dry quickly, help mix oil and water in products, and prevent bacteria growth but, in turn, may cause the hair to dry out

End Trim- Trimming or cutting the split or dead ends off of the hair so the remaining hair can be healthy

Fast- Abstaining from certain foods and drinks to achieve a particular goal

Fatty Alcohols- Alcohols derived from coconut and palm oil that add moisture to the hair, help detangle and thicken hair products.

Generational Curses- Curses that are passed down from generation to generation

Hair Follicles- a small glad that surrounds the root of the hair

Hair Porosity- How well the hair can retain moisture

Heat Damage- Damage to the hair strand caused by excessive heat from flat ironing or blow-drying

Hereditary Diseases- Diseases that have been passed down throughout generations

High Porosity- Cuticles can be too far apart that it soaks up moisture but loses it just as easy. This can be a result of too much hair processing like bleaching, blow-drying, etc.

Hydrogen Bonds- A protein structure in the hair that is easily broken by water or heat.

Hygiene- The way one cares for their body and hair

Hygral Fatigue- Water damage to the hair

Low Porosity- Cuticles on the hair shaft so close together that it may be hard for the hair to retain or soak up moisture

Lycopene- red pigment found in watermelon, tomatoes, and berries

Nutrient Rich Foods- foods that provide nourishment to the body that is needed to maintain life

ROOTS UNCOVERED

Product Build-up- The residue or accumulation of products on the hair

Protective Styles- Styles that keep the hair and ends of the hair protected from manipulation

Protein Conditioner- Conditioner that is used to strengthen hair by adding amino acids and protein.

Protein Structures- Protein Structures is what the hair is mainly made of. The hair consists of about 90% of keratin, which is a protein structure.

Regimen- A detailed plan designed to improve a specific area in a person's life

Relaxer- A cream used to relax or straighten curls chemically and permanently by breaking down the hair's disulfide bonds. A relaxer retouch is only applied to the new growth on previously relaxed hair.

Repentance- The act of asking God for forgiveness, changing your mind, changing your ways, and choosing not to return to them again

Reputable- Honorable; known for having good character or producing good work; trustworthy

Retain Length- Keep the length of the hair instead of it breaking

Sedentary Lifestyle- An inactive lifestyle

Telogen Phase- This is the resting phase in the hair growth cycle when the hair follicle is completely inactive, and it sheds to prepare for new hair. This phase tends to last about three months.

Texture- The type of curl pattern one has

Trichologist- Someone who specializes and treat the hair and scalp.

FOOD GUIDE

Listed below are popular foods that are beneficial for preventing hair loss and promoting hair growth.

Almonds promote hair growth, help prevent dandruff and hair damage. Almonds provide sufficient nutrition to the hair follicles that make the hair strands stronger, reducing hair loss

Bananas help block DHT and support the circulatory system in bringing vital nutrients into the scalp.

Carrots help block DHT, hair growth, and general scalp health.

Cashews halt testosterone from converting into DHT and contain large amounts of minerals that prompt hair regrowth.

Egg Yolks are a great source of biotin, which assists in growing healthy hair. They also help subdue DHT production.

Flax Seeds help block DHT and help remove dandruff and itching scalp.

Kale contains nutrients that stop testosterone

conversion into DHT and detoxifies excess hormones such as DHT from the body.

Mangos help reduce the conversion of testosterone into DHT. They assist in healing damaged scalps and brittle hair.

Oysters help block DHT production. They contain nutrients that provide proper blood circulation essential in carrying nutrients from the bloodstream to the hair follicles on the scalp.

Peanuts are full of biotin. They help block DHT and help increase hair growth.

Pecans help treat weak hair follicles due to scalp infections. They help reduce hair loss and scalp inflammation.

Pumpkin seeds help stop balding by blocking the build-up of DHT in the hair.

Soy contains nutrients that help promote hair growth and block DHT.

Tomatoes (Cooked and Dark) are a great source of the antioxidant lycopene, which stops testosterone from turning into DHT. Tomatoes help stop thinning and helps treat damaged hair follicles.

ROOTS UNCOVERED

Tuna is a great source of biotin, which helps prevent hair loss by slowing DHT production. Tuna also contains nutrients that help prevent dandruff, prevent inflammation, and promote hair growth.

Walnuts are high in protein and Vitamin E, helping increase hair growth and treating hair loss due to the prostate's medical problems.

Watermelon is an excellent natural DHT blocker full of minerals and vitamins that encourage hair growth.

White mushrooms are full of zinc, which blocks DHT production in the body. It also contains high sources of Vitamin D, which is vital for growing thick hairs on the scalp.

HAIR OIL GUIDE

Listed below are popular foods that are beneficial for preventing hair loss and promoting hair growth.

Argan Oil- Protects against heat and UV rays yet makes the hair shine. It moisturizes the hair making it more manageable.

Avocado Oil- Reduces dandruff, prevents breakage, helps detangle hair, protects from damage, promotes hair growth, and seals the hair.

Castor Oil- Promotes hair growth, helps prevent hair loss, moisturizes, coats, and protects the hair

Coconut Oil- Helps repair damaged and broken hair. It helps prevent hair loss and promotes healthy hair and scalp. It gives the hair shine and helps it retain moisture.

Flaxseed Oil- Helps prevent frizziness and breakage. Promotes hair growth and moisturizes the hair

Ginger Oil- soothes dry and itchy scalp, helps keep the scalp clean and healthy, promotes hair growth by stimulating the scalp

Grapeseed Oil- Helps fight dandruff, reduces scalp inflammation, blocks DHT, moisturizes hair, adds shine, and restores strength to hair

Jamaican Black Castor Oil- Moisturizes, strengthens, and increases the density of the hair. It stimulates the scalp increasing the speed of hair growth. It prevents breakage and dry scalp.

Jojoba Oil- Prevents dry scalp and dandruff, moisturizes the hair, and makes the hair soft.

Lavender Oil- Prevents hair loss, promotes hair growth, increases hair density, moisturizes the scalp

Olive Oil- Gives the hair shine, moisturizes, and protects against heat damage

Peppermint Oil- Promotes hair growth, increase blood circulation in the scalp

Rosemary Oil-Improves blood circulation, reduces dandruff build-up, promotes hair growth, heals nerve damage in the scalp, restores hair, protects against hair loss

Sweet Almond- Moisturizes, seals the hair, and protects against breakage and hair loss

Tea Tree Oil- helps fight dandruff build-up, unclog hair follicles, and promotes hair growth

QUANISHA WHITFIELD

AUTHOR BIO

Quanisha was raised in the small town of Engelhard, North Carolina, where she learned to value her faith above all other things. Full of ambition, she moved to Durham, North Carolina, to attend North Carolina Central University, where she attained a Bachelor's in Public Health Education. One month after graduation, she went on to attend Durham Beauty Academy. In 2017, she received a License in Cosmetology and is the founder and owner of Hannora LLC. She is passionate about Christ, the wellness of people, and healthy hair. She desired to merge the knowledge she has of Christ and her professions. Quanisha has discovered that some hair issues may be an issue of the scalp, an unhealthy diet, and an unhealthy soul. Her ultimate goal is to help people uncover, correct, and heal these areas so that they can attain healthy hair as well as a healthy body and soul.

REFERENCES

"Anagen." *Merriam-Webster.com Dictionary*, Merriam-Webster, **https://www.merriam-webster.com/dictionary/anagen**. Accessed 2 Apr. 2021.

"The Anatomy and Structure of Hair." *Dedicated to Shea Butter Training and Education*, **www.sheainstitute.com/asbi-library/hair-anatomy/#:~:text=%20The%20Anatomy%20and%20Structure%20of%20Hair%20,up%20of%20long%20proteins%20that%20twist...%20More%20**.

Becker, Tonya McKay. "Alcohols and Your Hair, What You Should Know." *NaturallyCurly.com*, 9 Apr. 2019, **www.naturallycurly.com/curlreading/curl-products/all-about-alcohols**.

"BIOTIN: Overview, Uses, Side Effects, Precautions, Interactions, Dosing, and Reviews." *WebMD*, WebMD, **www.webmd.com/vitamins/ai/ingredientmono-313/biotin**.

"Catagen." *Merriam-Webster.com Dictionary*, Merriam-Webster, **https://www.merriam-webster.com/dictionary/catagen**. Accessed 2 Apr. 2021.

"Hair Biology & Bonds." *Philip Kingsley*, **www.philipkingsley.com/hair-guide/hair-science/the-**

biology-of-your-hair/#:~:text=%E2%80%98Disulphide%20bonds%20are%20one%20of%20the%20strongest%20naturally-occurring,by%20chemical%20bonds%20called%20disulphide%20and%20hydrogen%20bonds.

Heather L. Brannon, MD. "How the Telogen Phase Can Cause Hair Loss." *Verywell Health*, 25 Aug. 2020, **www.verywellhealth.com/telogen-phase-1069283**.

Likelovedo, et al. "Drying Alcohols to Avoid in CG Method." *Like Love Do*, 10 June 2020, likelovedo.com/2020/04/drying-alcohols-to-avoid-in-cg-method/#:~:text=What%20are%20drying%20alcohols%20and%20why%20should%20we,essential%20moisture%20thus%20straightening%20curls%20and%20damaging%20hair.

"Vanessa Osbourne." *NaturallyCurly.com*, 1 Apr. 2016, **www.naturallycurly.com/texture-typing/hair-porosity**.

"What Is Androgenic Alopecia?" *WebMD*, WebMD, **www.webmd.com/skin-problems-and-treatments/hair-loss/qa/what-is-androgenic-alopecia**.

What You Need to Know About DHT and Hair Loss, **www.healthline.com/health/dht**.

"Trichologist." *Merriam-Webster.com Dictionary*, Merriam-Webster, **https://www.merriam-**

webster.com/dictionary/trichologist. Accessed 2 Apr. 2021.

www.ingramcontent.com/pod-product-compliance
Lightning Source LLC
Chambersburg PA
CBHW051705090426
42736CB00013B/2556